HIRAGANA
the Basics of Japanese

Clay & Yumi Boutwell

Published by Kotoba Books

Visit **http://www.TheJapanShop.com** for quality
Japanese language learning materials.

ISBN: 1481863088
ISBN-13: 978-1481863087

If you look at the chart on the front cover, you will notice the hiragana are grouped into sections by row. Most sections cover five hiragana. At the end of each section of this book, there are quizzes, games, and other exercises to aid memorization.

If you study one or two pages a day for ten to thirty minutes, you will learn hiragana in a few short weeks! AND you will begin reading Japanese—*real* Japanese—the first day!

You will have to work of course, but that's all part of the fun.

Let's begin the adventure —

HIRAGANA

Below are a few hints that will help make your learning process easier:

- Written Japanese is made of **kanji** (Chinese characters), **katakana** (Hiragana's sister which is used mainly for foreign words and names), and **hiragana**.

- Forty-six characters represent the Japanese sound system and, except for a few cases, each character's sound is unique [unlike English where five vowels (a,e,i,o, and u) represent fifteen vowel sounds!]

- A few additional sounds are made by combining two hiragana or by adding a " or a °. [More on this later.]

- Every hiragana, katakana, or kanji has a specific stroke order. This book shows the stroke order for all hiragana. Sometimes, however, characters with one stroke are shown in this book with two strokes for ease of understanding.

- Stroke order usually **starts from the upper left** corner down to the lower right. **Vertical lines** are drawn from **top to bottom** and **horizontal lines** are **left to right**. Knowing this, you can guess how to write most characters.

ABOUT THIS BOOKLET

We believe, studying regularly for fifteen minutes each day is far more effective than two hours once a week. Atop each page we have included space to record how much time you spend studying each day. Use it to encourage regular study time.

In the hiragana box to the right, we have the hiragana, its *romaji* (romanized / alphabet letters), and its approximate sound. There are also squares to practice writing. Print the downloadable PDF for more writing practice. Please follow the stroke order shown. Even if your goal is simply to read, knowing the correct stroke order will help you in other areas such as learning kanji and overall better writing.

romaji - a
sound - fAther

We also give memory tips for each character. Admittedly, some of them are pretty silly; but the sillier they are, the easier they stick. Give them a try, but feel free to come up with different memory tricks that work best for you.

FREE EXTRA RESOURCES

In the back of the book, you will find a link to download sound files and PDFs for printing extra writing practice sheets. We encourage you to download that now, print a few pages, and then turn the page to get started.

ねこ＆ねずみ
Cat & Mouse

Gambarimashou!
(Let's do our best!)
Clay & Yumi Boutwell

www.TheJapanShop.com
www.TheJapanesePage.com

Find other resources at our store: http://www.TheJapanShop.com

あ

romaji - a
sound - fAther

This is the first of the vowels. There are only **FIVE** vowel sounds. All the other characters are made of a **consonant** + a **vowel** (except the "n" sound)

Usually, you draw horizontally and then vertically, from top to bottom.

| 1 ﹁ | 2 す | 3 あ |

MEMORY HELP

A "t" with a slanted "g" makes an "**ah**" sound

| あ | あ | | | | | | | | |

い

romaji - i
sound - fEEt

| 1 レ | 2 い |

Now we come to our first real word.
Let's put あ together with い and see what happens!

あ + い = あい *ai* which means "**love!**"

Not a bad first day's work!

MEMORY HELP

It looks like two dangling f**EE**t!!

| い | い | | | | | | | | |

This hiragana is sometimes used to make other characters longer in duration. Actually, all the vowels work in this capacity, but う is probably the most used. We will cover this later, so don't worry about it now *but don't forget it either*!

romaji - u
sound - fOOd

MEMORY HELP

It looks like an open mouth looking for "f**OO**d"

It may seem difficult at first, but learning these first few hiragana will be the base for your Japanese future! Learn these important ones well.

Also, learn these in order [a, i, u, e, o].

romaji - e
sound - bEt
or sometimes like the letter A

MEMORY HELP

h**E**Y, it's a man running

TIP: Hiragana and Katakana are "syllabaries" and not alphabets; the symbols represent syllables: "ma" is one character in Japanese, but two letters in English.

お

romaji - o
sound - Oh nO!

Don't confuse this with あ!

一 お お

You are on your last hiragana vowel. Congratulations!

MEMORY HELP

It looks like "あ a" but **Oh!** it's different.

お | お | | | | | | | | |

You are doing fine! Now write the following in romaji.

HERE ARE SOME REAL JAPANESE WORDS
How do you pronounce them? Copy the hiragana.

あい _____ This means *love*

あおい _____ This means *blue*

え _____ This means *picture; painting*

いえ _____ This means *house*

おおい _____ This means *a lot* or *much* [Long お sound]

いいえ _____ This means *no* [Long い sound]

いう _____ This means *to talk*

いい _____ This means *good* [Long い sound]

Crossword Challenge!
Practice writing the hiragana (not romaji)!

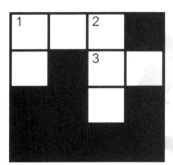

Across

1 This means "blue" (3)

3 This means "good" (2)

Down

1 This means "love" (2)

2 This means "no" (3)

Now, try to answer the following questions from memory.
(Of course, if you must peek, look above.)

Q&A:

1) あい means _____

2) How do you write "blue" in Japanese? _____

3) How would you say "blue house" in Japanese? [hint "blue" + "house"] _____

TRUE OR FALSE: (circle one)

1) いえ means "no"   T   F

2) あおい means "red"   T   F

Answers in back

か

romaji - ka
sound - CAr

Now that you have learned the vowels [あいうえお], let's build from them! The remaining hiragana (except one) are sounds we would write with two or more letters in English. This chapter begins the "k" row and this one [か] is "k" + "a" or "ka." (two letters but one hiragana character)

MEMORY HELP

It looks like a "K" with the top falling off

き

romaji - ki
sound - KEY

Continuing with the "k" section and adding the second vowel sound "i" we get "ki." The sound KI means "tree" in Japanese.

MEMORY HELP

It looks like a skeleton **KEY**

Katakana, hiragana's sister, is used primarily to write foreign words and names. Your name would be written in katakana.

Now we have "k" and the 3rd vowel "u" to make "*ku*" better known as the "less than" mark. When drawing this character, start at the top (right) go down left then finally down right.

romaji - ku
sound - COOl

MEMORY HELP

It looks like pa**KU** man (Pac-man™)

Perhaps now you can see how the rest of hiragana is constructed: a consonant + one of the five vowel sounds. No problem! The sound KE means "hair" in Japanese.

romaji - ke
sound - KEttle

MEMORY HELP

It looks like a broken old KEttle

TIP: Practice writing & recognizing hiragana here:
http://thejapanesepage.com/hiragana

こ

romaji - ko
sound - COla

Now that you have learned the vowel sounds and have studied the first consonant + vowel line, you should have a basic understanding of hiragana. But don't worry if you are still a bit confused... Getting used to the pattern takes time.

MEMORY HELP

It's obviously a "**CO**la can" with no sides...

こ こ

Let's get moving...

HERE ARE SOME REAL JAPANESE WORDS
How do you pronounce them? Copy the hiragana.

かお _____ This means *face*

えき _____ This means *train station*

おおきい _____ This means *big* [pronounce the O long]

いく _____ This means *to go*

くうこう _____ This means *airport* [the う makes the く and こ a longer sound. You don't pronounce it as

こい _____ This means *love* or *carp (fish)*

かき _____ This means *persimmon*

いけ _____ This means *pond*

Crossword Challenge!

Practice writing the hiragana (not romaji)!

Across

1 This means "face" (2)

3 This means "persimmon" (2)

4 This means "to go" (2)

Down

2 This means "big" (4)

Now, try to answer the following questions from memory.
(Of course, if you must peek look on the previous page.)

Q&A:

1) How do you write "big (train) station" [big + station]

___ ___ ___ ___   ___ ___

2) Which writing system is used for foreign names, hiragana or katakana? _____ [p.8]

TRUE OR FALSE: (circle one)

1) くうこう means "airport"   T   F

2) To make some sounds longer add an う   T   F

Answers in back

さ

romaji - sa
sound - SOlitude

This looks similar to き [p. 8] but with one less line.

Make drawing hiragana fun! The more you draw them the quicker you will remember them.

MEMORY HELP

It looks like a **SA**rgeant barking orders.

し

romaji - shi
sound - SHE

This is one of the least complicated to draw! Remember to always start at the top and go down when drawing Japanese characters. You may be expecting "*si*" but it is pronounced "*shi*."

MEMORY HELP

SHE has hair flowing in the wind.

When writing romaji, many Japanese write "*si*" for し. However, for the non-Japanese, "*shi*" is much closer to the pronunciation.

一 す

す

romaji - su
sound - SUE

For the second stroke: Start from the top and as you go down, loop it to the left and then end with a tail.

MEMORY HELP

It looks like a girl named **SUE** wearing a hat. uth.

す　す

一 ナ せ

せ

romaji - se
sound - SEt

Are you writing each character many times? Try to use more than one sense: seeing, speaking, and writing the characters aid memorization more than just seeing.

MEMORY HELP

An opened mouth person wearing a hat **SAY**ing something

せ　せ

TIP: You can immediately recongize hiragana from katakana by its more fluid form.

そ

romaji - so
sound - SO

ー フ そ

Another way to write this one is そ

Just remember that they are the same character.

MEMORY HELP

It looks **SO** abstract it could be
Pica**SO**

そ そ

HERE ARE SOME REAL JAPANESE WORDS
How do you pronounce them? Copy the hiragana.

さけ _____ This means *Japanese alcohol*

うし _____ This means *cow*

すし _____ This means *sushi*

あさ _____ This means *morning*

すき _____ This means *to like (something)*

うそ _____ This means *a lie*

かさ _____ This means *umbrella*

せき _____ This means *chair* or *to cough*

Crossword Challenge!
Practice writing the hiragana (not romaji)!

Across

2. This means "to like"

3. This means "cow"

Down

1. This means "chair"

2. This means "sushi"

3. This means "a lie"

Now, try to answer the following questions from memory.

Q&A:

1) How do you write sushi in hiragana?   ___ ___

2) How is かさ pronounced? _____

TRUE OR FALSE: (circle one)

1) さ is "*ki*" and き is "*sa*"   T   F

2) There are two ways to write そ   T   F

Answers in back

た

romaji - ta
sound - TOddler

一　ナ　た　た

You are now beginning the "t" row. You will encounter two irregular pronunciations. Until now, it has been pretty easy: one consonant + one vowel with no irregularities. Here's one more regular one.

MEMORY HELP

It looks like a **TO**ddler reaching for a toy

た　た

ち

romaji - chi
sound—CHEAp

一　ち

You should be congratulated! You have reached your first "irregular" hiragana pronunciation. Yeah! Ahem... This is pronounced "*chi*" and not "*ti*" as you would think.

MEMORY HELP

A **CHE**ap version of the number 5

ち　ち

There are a few irregular pronunciations in hiragana. The front and back charts show these in red.

TSU. This one is a bit difficult to pronounce. The sound is NOT found in English. But if you say the words "cat" and "soup" fast you get a caTSOUp. This is the sound you want.

Later, we will see a small つ. This causes a short pause between syllables.

romaji - tsu
sound - caT SOUp

MEMORY HELP

A wave from a **TSU**nami (tidal wave)

Taking a break from the irregular, let's continue on with what you are used to. By the way, "hand" in Japanese is *te*. (KaraTE—empty hand)

romaji - te
sound - TErrible

MEMORY HELP

A **TE**rrible 7

Listen to a native speaker or download the sound files from the back of the book to hear the つ *tsu* sound.

と

romaji - to
sound - TOE

| 1 | 2 と |

You have finished the fourth row. You are getting close to the mid mark—don't give up. You are doing just fine!

MEMORY HELP

It looks like someone's big **TOE**

| と | と | | | | | | | | | |

HERE ARE SOME REAL JAPANESE WORDS
How do you pronounce them? Copy the hiragana.

おと _____ This means *sound*

とおい _____ This means *far*

いち _____ This means *the number 1*

ちち _____ This means *father*

すてき _____ This means *nice*

さとう _____ This means *sugar* (the う makes と

くち _____ This means *mouth*

うた _____ This means *song*

Crossword Challenge!

Practice writing the hiragana (not romaji)!

Across

   2 This means "far" (3)

   4 This means "father" (2)

Down

   1 This means "sound" (2)

   3 This means "1" (2)

Now, try to answer the following questions from memory.

Q&A:

1) Write the two hiragana with irregular pronunciations in this chapter ___ ___

2) How do you write "song" in Japanese? _____

TRUE OR FALSE: (circle one)

1) いち means "2"   T   F

2) すてき means "steak"   T   F

Answers in back

な

1	2	3	4
一	ナ	ナ	な

romaji - na
sound - kNOt

There are three characters that have a 厶 part. They are all in the "n" section.

MEMORY HELP

It looks like a rope all tangled in a kNOt

な	な								

に

1	2	3
⎸	⎸ー	に

romaji - ni
sound - knee

Try your best to learn to read **and** write hiragana. Even Japanese, when they forget a kanji (Chinese character) can always write the word in hiragana.

MEMORY HELP

It looks like a person sitting on his **kNEE**s (as seen from above)

に	に								

To learn basic Japanese grammar, go to
www.thejapanesepage.com/grammar

Here is the second ね character. We are pointing this out because there are several characters that have a similar look.

romaji - nu
sound - NEw

MEMORY HELP

It looks like an あ but it has a tail and no hat—a **NEW** *nu*

ぬ ぬ

There will be two more hiragana that look similar to ね. Be sure to get straight that "*ne*" is the one with the tail— ね

romaji - ne
sound - NEck

MEMORY HELP

If you look carefully you will see a "1," "+," and a "2," but, **NAY**, no "3."

ね ね

ね is also used as a sentence ending particle. It has a very versatile meaning: "isn't it?", "don't you?", and "you know…"

の

romaji - no
sound - NO

| 1 | 1b |
| 1 | の |

This hiragana is used as a particle [grammatical marker] as well as a part of a word. As a particle, it is the possessive (apostrophe S)

ねこ　の　えさ
cat　's　food

MEMORY HELP

A 9 on its side. [German for **NO** is "nein" pronounced "nine"]

| の | の | | | | | | | | | |

HERE ARE SOME REAL JAPANESE WORDS
How do you pronounce them? Copy the hiragana.

ねこ _____ This means *cat*

この _____ This means *this*

ねつ _____ This means *fever*

いぬ _____ This means *dog*

にし _____ This means *West*

なつ _____ This means *summer*

なに _____ This means *what*

なな _____ This means *seven*

Crossword Challenge!

Practice writing the hiragana (not romaji)!

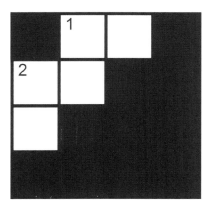

Across

1. This means "cat"

2. This means "summer"

Down

1. This means "fever"

2. This means "what?"

Find home: Follow the hiragana in order to get home and out of the maze

	い	き	し	つ	の	お	な	つ
の	と	て	に	ぬ	お	さ	あ	う
ね	な	つ	ち	い	す	こ	け	お
ぬ	に	う	た	と	ぬ	の	に	て
て	け	し	そ	あ	う	え	お	さ
い	こ	ね	せ	あ	い	に	か	ね
ぬ	き	お	す	し	な	と	き	そ
あ	く	な	に	さ	こ	け	く	す
し	の	と	さ	す	の	と	つ	ぬ

は

romaji - ha
sound - HA!

1	2	3	3b
い	にー	けさ	は

This and "he" [see page 25] are the only hiragana that have two sounds for one character. When "は" is used to make up words like はし *hashi* (chopsticks) it is pronounced "**ha**." However when used as a grammatical marker (as the topic marker), it is pronounced "**WA.**"

MEMORY HELP

It has two parts to make memorizing **HA**rd.

は	は								

ひ

romaji - hi
sound - HE

1	1b	1c
⌐	て	ひ

Nearly every letter in the English alphabet has two or more possible sounds, but remarkably, Japanese sounds and characters are very regular.

MEMORY HELP

It looks like a smiley face saying "**HEE HEE**"

ひ	ひ								

NOTE: Japanese children learn hiragana before learning katakana or kanji.

ふ

romaji - fu
sound - FOOd

| 1 ` | 2 ろ | 3 ふ | 4 ふ |

This can also be written as ふ

Just remember that the middle line can be drawn or not. Also the pronunciation of this is not "*hu*" as you would expect but "*fu*." As in とうふ *toufu*—tofu. Although, the sound is sometimes in-between "*hu*" and "*fu*."

MEMORY HELP

It looks like a snake looking for some **FOO**d

ふ | ふ | | | | | | | | | |

へ

romaji - he
sound - [a short] HEAd

| 1 ✓ | 1b へ | 1c へ |

"へ" can be pronounced as "*he*" or "*e*." Usually, when used as part of a word, it is pronounced as "*he*" as in へそ *heso* (belly button). And when used as a grammatical particle (to show direction) it is pronounced "*e*" —but not always!

MEMORY HELP

HEY! It's an upside V *(almost)*

へ | へ | | | | | | | | | |

You may see some hiragana drawn differently. English also has this:

[**a** or a]   [**m** or M]

ほ

romaji - ho
sound - HOle

| ¹ い | ² に | ³ に | ⁴ ほ |

This comes after は so it has a top bar. Notice the second bar is slightly longer than the first.

MEMORY HELP

HO OH! It is more complicated than は *ha*

| ほ | ほ | | | | | | | | |

HERE ARE SOME REAL JAPANESE WORDS
How do you pronounce them? Copy the hiragana.

はこ _____ This means *box*

ひと _____ This means *person*

ふね _____ This means *boat*

へた _____ This means *bad at,* or *unskilled*

はと _____ This means *dove*

ひたち _____ This means *Hitachi* (the company)

ほし _____ This means a *star*

とうふ _____ This means *tofu*
[the う just makes the と longer. You don't actually pronounce the う -- but a long と]

Crossword Challenge!

Practice writing the hiragana (not romaji)!

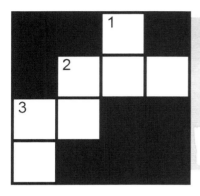

Across

2. This means "Hitachi"

3. This means "dove"

Down

1. This means "unskilled"

2. This means "person"

3. This means "box"

Now let's play a traditional Japanese game—Shiritori. "shiri" means "butt" and "tori" means "to catch." Someone starts with a word and the next player says another word that begins with the last letter of the previous word. Let's play Shiritori with a few words you have studied:

"box"　　　　　　は　こ　　　　　[p. 26]

"love" or "carp"　こ　___　　　　[p. 10]

"to go"　　　　　___　___　　　　[p. 10]

"airport"　　　　___　___　___　___　　　[p. 10]

"cow"　　　　　___　し　　　　　[p. 14]

Answers in back

ま

romaji - ma
sound - MA MA

一 二 ま ま

At first you may have to think of each memory help in order to say the pronunciation, but after a while, you will be able to simply look at the character and, *skipping the memory help*, your mind will jump right to the sound. This is real progress.

MEMORY HELP

Look **MA**! I caught a dragonfly. (Imagine a dragonfly)

ま　ま

み

romaji - mi
sound - ME

ㄱ み み

Also, there may be a few hiragana you know better than others. Don't let this worry you. In time as you read more and more, the bumps will be smoothed out.

MEMORY HELP

It looks to **ME** like a 2 over a 4

み　み

Hiragana (and katakana) originally came from kanji (Chinese characters).

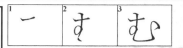

romaji - mu
sound - MOvie

Getting this far, you have accomplished quite a lot. Go on a treasure hunt on the internet. Start at a Japanese site such as *kids.yahoo.co.jp*. Find and sound out the hiragana you have studied.

MEMORY HELP

It looks like an old film projector showing a **MO**vie

Here we have the last of the look-a-likes.

romaji - me
sound - MEn

め [*me*] looks a lot like ぬ [*nu*], の [*no*], and even あ [*a*].

MEMORY HELP

It looks like a half closed eye. [in Japanese "eye" is "め"]

Also with *Yahoo Japan*, when you put your mouse over any link and look at the bottom, you will see the directory name in English!

も

romaji - mo
sound - MOWer

1	2	3
し	も	も

Now that you are finishing your seventh row, be sure to spend some time reviewing what you have studied.

MEMORY HELP

A man with a hat resting after MOwing his yard

も	も								

HERE ARE SOME REAL JAPANESE WORDS

How do you pronounce them? Copy the hiragana.

もも _____ This means *peach*

まめ _____ This means *bean*

ひみつ _____ This means *secret*

しまうま _____ This means *zebra* [the う does NOT make

たま _____ This means *ball*

まち _____ This means *town*

こめ _____ This means *rice*

さめ _____ This means *shark*

Crossword Challenge!

Practice writing the hiragana (not romaji)!

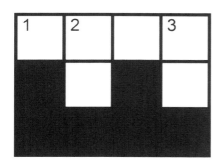

Across

1. This means "zebra"

Down

2. This means "beans"

3. This means "town"

Now, try to answer the following questions from memory.

Q&A:

1) How do you pronounce ぬ ___ & how do you pronounce め___?

2) Write *shimauma* [zebra] in Japanese. _____

TRUE OR FALSE: (circle one)

1) Hiragana came from kanji
   T   F

2) The correct order for the m's is もめむみま
   T   F

Answers in back

romaji - ya
sound - **YA**cht

If you look at the order of hiragana on the front of this booklet, you will see that the やゆよ row is missing a few sounds.

MEMORY HELP

A **YA**cht with its sail blowing in the wind

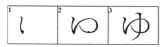

romaji - yu
sound - **YOU**

There is no *yi* or *ye* sound. That is why we are on *yu* now.

MEMORY HELP

If you look closely you may see a **y**, **o**, and a **u**

The "y" row has only *ya*, *yu* and *yo*.

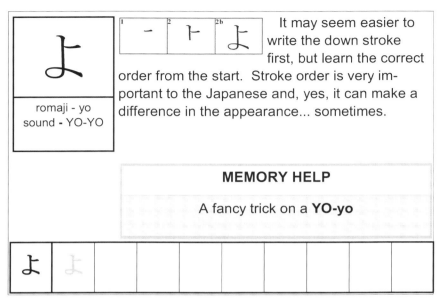

romaji - yo
sound - YO-YO

It may seem easier to write the down stroke first, but learn the correct order from the start. Stroke order is very important to the Japanese and, yes, it can make a difference in the appearance... sometimes.

MEMORY HELP

A fancy trick on a **YO-yo**

The や, ゆ, and よ can be used in two ways:
1) as "letters" to make words
2) or…

Take a look at the lower back cover where it says "plus small やゆ よ." Remember not to panic and then come back here. It looks scary but, really, it isn't too complicated.

There is a pattern.

In every case, a consonant sound is combined with a small や ya, ゆ yu, or よ yo. And the consonant sound has already been decided for you! It is always those under the "i" column. Look at the chart on the front or back (left) cover. Starting with the "k" row, we see き, し, ち, に, ひ, み, and り are used. (all i's)

Now, notice the sound changes. き ki + や ya = きゃ kya

Easy isn't it? You can think of the smaller や, ゆ, or よ as taking away the "i" sound in the first character. You may be saying, "What is the difference between きや kiya and きゃ kya?" First, the sound is different. "KI YA" (two syllables) versus "KYA" (one syllable). Second, the meaning can be totally different.

HERE ARE SOME REAL JAPANESE WORDS
How do you pronounce them?

はやい _____ This means *fast*

いきましょう _____ This means *let's go!*

へや _____ This means *room*

かいしゃ _____ This means *company; business*

おちゃ _____ This means *Japanese tea*

きょう _____ This means *today*

ひゃく _____ This means *hundred (100)*

Copy the following words to make a [*not so useful*] sentence in Japanese:

きょう、 _____ [the 、 is a comma]

きょう、あなた _____

きょう、あなたは _____

きょう、あなたは　ひゃく _____

きょう、あなたは　ひゃく　さい。_____

きょう–today
あなた–you [pronoun]
は *wa*–makes the preceding word or phrase the "topic" or "main thought" [not translated] (p. 24)
ひゃく–100
さい–years old

Now use the glossary to the left to figure out the meaning in English: [add an "are" in there]

_____

_____

Answer in back

Let's practice the small やゆよ

The following table shows all the hiragana you have learned with a small や, ゆ or よ. The last line [r line] will be studied next.

き+y	きゃ kya	きゅ kyu	きょ kyo
し+y	しゃ sha	しゅ shu	しょ sho
ち+y	ちゃ cha	ちゅ chu	ちょ cho
に+y	にゃ nya	にゅ nyu	にょ nyo
ひ+y	ひゃ hya	ひゅ hyu	ひょ hyo
み+y	みゃ mya	みゅ myu	みょ myo
り+y	りゃ rya	りゅ ryu	りょ ryo

NOTE: We didn't write the し and ち rows with a "y" in the romaji. If we were to write *sya* (as many Japanese people do) the sound to the foreign-er will be different. Both ways are correct—One being more "correct" to the Japanese understanding of the writing system and the other being more "correct" to the pronunciation.

Write "190" in Japanese

To write 190 in Japanese, you need to write **100** and **9** and **10**.

100	9	10
hyaku	*kyuu*	*juu*

[Remember to use う to make the *kyu* and *ju* longer; We will write "*ju*" since we haven't covered that yet.]

じゅ

_____   _____   _____
  hya ku   kyu u   ju u

ら

romaji - ra

You will notice there is no sound given for the "r" section. That is because the Japanese R sounds are different from any English sound. In this chapter, we will try to explain how to make the sounds [p 39], but be sure to listen to the sound files. ［See bottom］

MEMORY HELP

A 5 with a **RO**tten top

ら	ら										

り

romaji - ri

The R sound is in-between the R and L sounds in English.
Sometimes it sounds like a "D" to English ears. Pronunciation-wise this is the most difficult section, so learn it well. Once you get the hang of it, you will be understood.

MEMORY HELP

It looks like two arms **RE**aching for something

り	り										

For more info on how to correctly make the "r" sounds (with sound files), please visit **http://thejapanesepage.com/beginners/pronunciation**

る

| ¹ ⌐ | ² ろ | ³ る |

romaji - ru

If you have Japanese friends, ask them to help you with the "r" sounds. Listen carefully and mimic the sounds.

MEMORY HELP

It looks like a **ROO**t

| る | る | | | | | | | | |

れ

| ¹ ⏐ | ² わ | ³ れ |

romaji - re

Don't confuse this with
ね *ne* [p. 21]

MEMORY HELP

It is a snake **RE**sting on a stick

| れ | れ | | | | | | | | |

See next page for an overview on making "r" sounds.

ろ

romaji - ro

You have survived the last of the dreaded "r's"

Congratulations!

1	2
ろ	ろ

Spend some time listening to the sound files [see the last page for the download link] and reading page 39 to get your pronunciation down.

MEMORY HELP

Think of a man **ROW**ing a boat

ろ	ろ							

HERE ARE SOME REAL JAPANESE WORDS
How do you pronounce them? Copy the hiragana.

りか _____ This means *science*

らく _____ This means *easy*

くり _____ This means *chestnut*

りす _____ This means *squirrel*

あり _____ This means *ant*

あれ _____ This means *that*

れつ _____ This means *line*

ろうそく _____ This means *candle*

Overview of R sounds

There are two considerations for mastering the R's: **Tongue** and **Mouth**

PART ONE: The Tongue...

The sound is made by lightly slapping your tongue just behind your upper teeth. Think of making an L sound, like LOVE. That is the approximate place. The only difference between the Japanese R and the English L sound is how long the tongue is held there. In English the tongue is held a while so air can go around it. In Japanese, the tongue is immediately dropped. All of the R sounds are made the same way with the tongue.

PART TWO: The Mouth...

The mouth takes a little practice to make it natural, but it is also easy, really. Very simply, for RA RI & RE the mouth is more open and for RU & RO the mouth is more rounded and shut. [NOTE: actually for perfect pronunciation, ALL five sounds have unique mouth positions, but remember basically for RA, RI & RE the mouth is more opened and RU & RO it is rounded and smaller.]

RA	*RI*	*RU*	*RE*	*RO*
open wide	open wide	**round**	open wide	**round**

Again the most important thing is that RA, RI & RE have a kind of open, wide mouth and RU & RO have a more rounded, small mouth. Practice saying them in order -- (open mouth) RA RI (round mouth) RU (open mouth) RE (round mouth) RO.

Lastly, remember, slap the tongue with a wide mouth for RA, RI, RE and slap the tongue with a round mouth for RU & RO.

わ

romaji - wa
sound - WAsh

| 1 丨 | 2 才 | 3 わ |

There are only two letters under the "w" section. This is the only character that has a "w" sound. The next hiragana を is technically a "wo" but most of the time it is pronounced "o."

MEMORY HELP

It is a **WA**shing machine

わ	わ								

を

romaji - o
sound - OH

| 1 一 | 2 ナ | 3 を |

This character is **only** used as a grammatical particle. It will never be found as part of a word. You have studied the character that does that (お). を is placed right after the direct object. (see exercise at bottom of page 41)

MEMORY HELP

It looks like a person carefully stepping into a cold pond—**OH!** It's cold!

を	を								

を is the only hiragana that cannot be used to make words.

ん

romaji - n
sound - n or m

Finally the last one! This is the only one that has just one consonant sound—n. Also the ん **cannot** be used at the beginning of a word.

MEMORY HELP

It looks like a cursive "n" — *n*

ん | ん | | | | | | | | |

Copy the following words to make a sentence in Japanese:

わたし　　　_____

わたしは　　　_____

わたしは　ほん　_____

わたしは　ほんを　_____

わたしは　ほんを　よみたい。

_____

watashi–I (pronoun)
は　*wa*–makes the preceding word or phrase the "topic" or "main thought" [not translated] (p. 24)
hon–book
を　*O*–marks the Direct Object of the sentence [not translated]
yomitai–want to read

Now use the glossary to the left to figure out the meaning in English: [verb is last]

_____

_____

Answer in back

Small やゆよ review

The "i" column [き し ち に ひ み り] is combined with a small や, ゆ or よ to make additional sounds.

Write the hiragana for the following words:

1) *kyu u ri* _____ _____ _____ [cucumber]

2) *sho u ri* _____ _____ _____ [victory]

3) *o cha* _____ _____ [Japanese tea]

4) *ryo u ri* _____ _____ _____ [cooking, food]

5) *kyo u* _____ _____ [today]

6) *sha shi n* _____ _____ _____ [photo]

Answers in back

The small つ

Way back on page 17, we mentioned sometimes a small つ *tsu* is used to cause a short pause or break between syllables. For example, in English we have a slight pause after "black" in "blac**k ca**r." Here is a good example to show how important this small つ is.

がっき   *gakki* - musical instrument [with a slight pause]
and

がき   *gaki* - brat, annoying kid [without the pause]

Remember:
The small つ is not pronounced, but causes a short hiccup between sounds

Now here is what you have been waiting for. I am sure you have been wondering what those ゙ and ゚ things are all about. Although it isn't as easy as the little や, ゆ or よ's, again, there is a pattern that can be followed.

゙ The " or *"ten ten"* makes a soft sound harder. For example, it makes a "k" sound a hard "g" sound ("g" as in **g**ood). "s" becomes "z," "t" becomes "d," and "h" becomes "b."

゚ The ° or *"maru"* makes the "h" become a "p" sound. The other consonant sounds are not affected by the *maru*, only the "h" group. That's all there is to it!

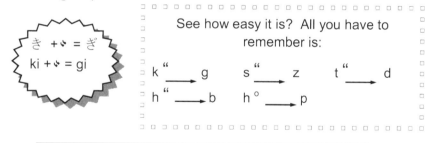

き + ゙ = ぎ
ki + ゙ = gi

See how easy it is? All you have to remember is:

k " → g   s " → z   t " → d

h " → b   h ° → p

Before doing the practice below, look at the chart on the back cover until you understand how it works.

Let's practice writing words with the " and the °

ω Here is き *ki*. How do you make a *gi*? _____

ω Here is ふ *fu*. How do you make a *pu*? _____

ω Here is きゆ *kyu*. How do you make a *gyu*? _____

ω Here is しよ *sho*. How do you make a *jo*? _____ *[look at chart]*

ω Now write *bi ji n*. This means "beautiful woman": _____

Answers in back

When か is given a *ten ten* [が], it can be a grammatical particle. (it can also be a regular "letter" to make up words…) As a grammatical particle it marks the subject of the sentence. Very often the usage of the particles は and が are similar. は usually covers a broad topic while が is more narrow.

Other particles:

は *wa*—topic marker   [as a regular "letter" it is pronounced "*ha*"]

へ *he* or *e*—directional marker

を *o*—direct object marker

が *ga*—subject marker

There are two sets with the same pronunciation with the *ten ten*. じ & ぢ are both pronounced *ji* and ず & づ are both **zu**. While all four characters do appear in words (and are not interchangeable) the じ **is more common than ぢ and the ず is more common than づ.** Think of *ji* as じ and *zu* as ず.

What's this in romaji?	**What's this in hiragana?**
じ = *ji*	*ji* = じ or ぢ
1. ぶ = _____	1. *ba* = _____
2. ぷ = _____	2. *do* = _____
3. だ = _____	3. *gu* = _____
4. びゃ = _____	4. *cho* = _____
5. づ = _____	5. *myu* = _____

Answer in back

FUN WITH **HIRAGANA**

I want you to meet Mr. *Henohenomoheji*

The name sounds impossible to remember, but it is simply reading the hiragana that makes the character. The eyebrow is "*he*." The eye is "*no*." The nose is "*mo*." the mouth is "he." And the face is made by "*ji*." (*ji* = *shi* + ") Do you see it? Try to draw it. Impress your friends.

Here's another one. Can you read it? It is also *henohenomoheji* but as a cat.

SHIRITORI - A traditional Japanese game which you have already seen (p. 27) is called *Shiritori*. If you remember, the game starts with someone saying a word. The next player takes the last "letter" of that word and uses it to begin the next word. *Shiritori* is an excellent way to have fun while gaining a larger vocabulary.

KAIBUN (Japanese palindrome) - This is a word play where a sentence can be read from the left or right and still make sense.

わたしまけましたわ   *watashi makemashita wa*—

Reading from either the left or right it means "I lost." [*watashi* = I; *makemashita* = lost; *wa* = sigh or exclamation sound] Notice this doesn't work looking at the romaji, but only with hiragana.

たけやぶやけた   *takeyabu yaketa*—Again reading from the left or the right, it means, "the bamboo grove burned." [*takeyabu* = bamboo grove; *yaketa* = was burned]

Yumi's challenge

Here is your chance to show off your awesome skills. Yumi has prepared a few sentences based mainly on words found in this booklet. See if you can sound out the words **and** understand them.

① りすは　くりが　すき。

② うしは　かおが　おおきい。

③ おおきい　くうこうへ　いきましょう。

④ しまうまは　はやい　です。

⑤ わたしは　えが　へた　です。

Some hints

➡️　は,　へ and が are used also as grammatical particles. [p. 44]

➡️　Japanese verbs are at the end of the sentence.

➡️　Think of です as "to be" [is, am, are]

Here are the page numbers for each word, if you need to look them up:
1) 38, 38, 14
2) 14, 10, 10
3) 10, 10, 34
4) 30, 34, *desu*
5) 41, 6, 26, *desu*

HIRAGANA
PRACTICE PAD

ひらがな

DATE: _____ 48 TIME SPENT: _____

Hiragana Practice Pad

あ	あ								
あ	あ								
あ	あ								
あ	あ								

い	い								
い	い								
い	い								
い	い								

Hiragana Practice Pad

う　う
う　う
う　う
う　う

え　え
え　え
え　え
え　え

お	お								
お	お								
お	お								
お	お								

か	か								
か	か								
か	か								
か	か								

Hiragana Practice Pad

き	き								
き	き								
き	き								
き	き								

く	く								
く	く								
く	く								
く	く								

DATE: _____ 52 TIME SPENT: _____

Hiragana Practice Pad

け	け								
け	け								
け	け								
け	け								

こ	こ								
こ	こ								
こ	こ								
こ	こ								

DATE: _____ 53 TIME SPENT: _____

Hiragana Practice Pad

さ	さ								
さ	さ								
さ	さ								
さ	さ								

し	し								
し	し								
し	し								
し	し								

Hiragana Practice Pad

す

せ

す	す								
す	す								
す	す								
す	す								

せ	せ								
せ	せ								
せ	せ								
せ	せ								

DATE: _____ 55 TIME SPENT: _____

Hiragana Practice Pad

そ	そ								
そ	そ								
そ	そ								
そ	そ								

た	た								
た	た								
た	た								
た	た								

Hiragana Practice Pad

ち	ち								
ち	ち								
ち	ち								
ち	ち								

つ	つ								
つ	つ								
つ	つ								
つ	つ								

DATE: _____ 57 TIME SPENT: _____

Hiragana Practice Pad

て	て								
て	て								
て	て								
て	て								

と	と								
と	と								
と	と								
と	と								

Hiragana Practice Pad

な	な								
な	な								
な	な								
な	な								

に	に								
に	に								
に	に								
に	に								

ぬ

ね

Hiragana Practice Pad

ぬ	ぬ								
ぬ	ぬ								
ぬ	ぬ								
ぬ	ぬ								

ね	ね								
ね	ね								
ね	ね								
ね	ね								

DATE: _____ 60 TIME SPENT: _____

Hiragana Practice Pad

の	の								
の	の								
の	の								
の	の								

は	は								
は	は								
は	は								
は	は								

ひ

ふ

Hiragana Practice Pad

ひ	ひ								
ひ	ひ								
ひ	ひ								
ひ	ひ								

ふ	ふ								
ふ	ふ								
ふ	ふ								
ふ	ふ								

へ	へ								
へ	へ								
へ	へ								
へ	へ								

ほ	ほ								
ほ	ほ								
ほ	ほ								
ほ	ほ								

DATE: _____ 63 TIME SPENT: _____

Hiragana Practice Pad

ま	ま							
ま	ま							
ま	ま							
ま	ま							

み	み							
み	み							
み	み							
み	み							

DATE: _____ 64 TIME SPENT: _____

Hiragana Practice Pad

む	む								
む	む								
む	む								
む	む								

め	め								
め	め								
め	め								
め	め								

Hiragana Practice Pad

も	も								
も	も								
も	も								
も	も								

や	や								
や	や								
や	や								
や	や								

Hiragana Practice Pad

ゆ	ゆ								
ゆ	ゆ								
ゆ	ゆ								
ゆ	ゆ								

よ	よ								
よ	よ								
よ	よ								
よ	よ								

DATE: _____ 67 TIME SPENT: _____

Hiragana Practice Pad

ら	ら								
ら	ら								
ら	ら								
ら	ら								

り	り								
り	り								
り	り								
り	り								

Hiragana Practice Pad

る	る								
る	る								
る	る								
る	る								

れ	れ								
れ	れ								
れ	れ								
れ	れ								

ろ	ろ								
ろ	ろ								
ろ	ろ								
ろ	ろ								

わ	わ								
わ	わ								
わ	わ								
わ	わ								

DATE: _____ 70 TIME SPENT: _____

Hiragana Practice Pad

を	を								
を	を								
を	を								
を	を								

ん	ん								
ん	ん								
ん	ん								
ん	ん								

FREE PRACTICE

FREE PRACTICE

FREE PRACTICE

FREE PRACTICE

ANSWERS: Crosswords

P. 7

あ	お	²い	
い		³い	い
		え	

P. 11

か	²お	
	お	
³か	き	
⁴い	く	

P. 15

	¹せ	
²す	き	
³う	し	
そ		

P. 19

¹お		
²と	お	³い
		⁴ち	ち

P. 23

	⁴ね	こ
²な	つ	
に		

P. 27

		¹へ	
	²ひ	た	ち
³は	と		
こ			

P. 23

P. 31

¹し	²ま	う	³ま
	め		ち

ANSWERS: Questions

P. 7 - Q&A 1) love 2) あおい 3) あおい　いえ　T/F　1) F [いいえ is no] 2) F [あおい is blue]

P. 11 - Q&A 1) おおきい　えき　2) katakana　T/F　1) T 2) T

P. 15 - Q&A 1) すし 2) ka sa [means "umbrella"] T/F　1) F [さ is "sa"; き is "ki"] 2) T

P. 19 - Q&A 1) ち chi & つ tsu 2) うた T/F　1) F [いち means "1"] 2) F [すてき means "nice"]

P. 27 - box = はこ; love or carp = こい; to go = いく; airport = くうこう; cow = うし

P. 31 - Q&A 1) ぬ nu め me 2) しまうま T/F　1) T 2) F [まみむめも]

P. 34 - きょう、あなたはひゃくさい。 means "Today, you *are* a hundred years old."

P. 35 - ひゃく　きゅう　じゅう

P. 41 - わたしはほんをよみたい。 means "I want to read a book."

P. 42 - 1) きゅうり　2) しょうり　3) おちゃ　4) りょうり　5) きょう　6) しゃしん

P. 43 - 1) ぎ　gi 2) ぷ pu 3) ぎゅ gyu 4) じょ jo 5) びじん bijin

P. 44 - romaji 1) bu 2) pu 3) da 4) bya 5) zu　hiragana 1) ば　2) ど　3) ぐ　4) ちょ 5) みゅ

FREE EXTRA RESOURCES

To get a download that includes all the Hiragana sounds and a PDF for printing extra writing practices, please type the following URL in the browser on your computer:

http://TheJapanesePage.com/downloads/hiraganaextras.zip

If you have any problems with the download or have any other questions, please email us at help@thejapanshop.com.

どうもありがとうございました！

Made in the USA
San Bernardino, CA
22 June 2013